GENERATIVE AI

Comprehensive Guide for Beginners

Table of Contents

HERE IS YOU FREE GIFT!

You will find:

1. Pills from Generative AI

2 All the best Generative AIs

3. The future of Generative AI

4. _Personalizing your own Generative AI

5. ....and more

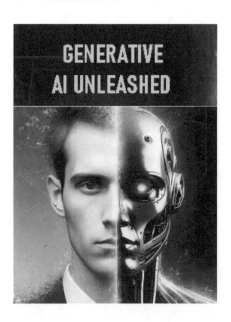

PLEASE SCAN QR CODE
FOR YOUR IMMEDIATE
QUICK FIRST BONUS
ACCESS

for free

INTRODUCTION

Innovation, evolution, and future technologies have driven advancements throughout human history. The innovation of the internet has transformed the ways in which we socialize, impacting our lifestyles, interactions, and relationships. Currently, several emerging technologies stand poised to significantly influence human lives and businesses.

Artificial Intelligence, commonly known as AI, is one of the rapidly advancing technologies that has enhanced the quality of life by improving everyday routines and tackling complex tasks more efficiently than humans. This improvement makes life easier, safer, and more productive.

Artificial Intelligence (AI) involves creating machines capable of performing operations that typically require human intelligence and effort, such as recognizing speech or making decisions. According to Tech Target, "Artificial Intelligence is the simulation of human intelligence processes by machines, especially computer systems. Specific applications of AI include expert systems, natural language processing, speech recognition, and machine vision."

AI has been widely used across various business sectors, from healthcare and finance to the food industry, transportation, construction, and numerous others. It is speculated that future AI could alter how we function and communicate.

Mike Thomas, a senior feature writer at Built, notes, "AI's impact on technology is profound as it influences computation. Through Artificial Intelligence, machines can store vast quantities of data and use their intelligence to make excellent judgments and findings in a fraction of the time it would take humans."

With artificial intelligence, individuals can make better decisions and analyze information that is nearly impossible for humans to find on their own. AI also automates several difficult and time-consuming tasks, allowing humans to focus on more resourceful and creative endeavors.

ChatGPT, a language model developed by OpenAI in 2022, is an example of an artificial intelligence tool. According to Sabrina Oan, Associate Editor at Sabrina Ortiz ZEDNET, "ChatGPT is an intuitive language tool powered by AI technology that enables human-like conversations and much more. The language model can answer questions and assist with tasks such as crafting essays, emails, and code."

As Sabrina stated, ChatGPT is designed to help humans engage in essential discussions, providing advice, answering various questions people may have, and generating creative articles. ChatGPT has assisted many creators in generating strategic content ideas for their businesses in less time. Industries have harnessed the power of ChatGPT for consumer services applications, where consumers receive clarification to their challenges and questions without waiting for human responses.

On the other hand, the Metaverse is a virtual world created by the convergence of physical and virtual reality. Although the concept has been around for some time, it has recently gained more attention due to the increasing interest in virtual and augmented reality technologies.

The Metaverse is a communal space where humans can interact with one another and automate objects simultaneously using artificial intelligence and augmented reality technologies. The impact of the Metaverse on human lives and businesses is profound, offering a new way for human-to-human communication. Instead of traditional chatting and video communication, people now have the ability to interact in a virtual environment that is more captivating and engaging. Moreover, the Metaverse allows participation in distant events that may not be accessible in the physical world.

The revolution of the Metaverse creates new opportunities for businesses to reach more customers and engage with them in better and quicker ways. For instance, an e-commerce website enabling people to buy and sell digital and physical products online has relieved many small business owners of the stress of maintaining a brick-and-mortar store, ultimately generating more profit for their businesses.

In conclusion, the impact of AI, ChatGPT, and the Metaverse on human lives cannot be overstated.

CHAPTER 1: THE POWER OF AI NOWADAYS: WHAT AI CAN DO FOR HUMANS

Artificial Intelligence (AI) is a powerful tool transforming human communication, interaction, human behavior, and access to the world around us.

The "Oxford Dictionary" defines Artificial Intelligence as the idea and evolution of information processing systems that can execute duties generally requiring human intelligence, such as optical perception, speech recognition, decision-making, and language translation. AI has gone beyond the technical advantage to help in our day-to-day activities, such as assisting us in our businesses, how we relate and communicate with people, how we provide solutions to problems, and making life-changing decisions within a short period.

Artificial Intelligence (AI) has brought refreshing opportunities to humanity and made life easier in every sector. This capability has opened up a world of possibilities, from predicting weather patterns to developing new drugs to detecting fraud. In this chapter, I will show you some of the ways and sectors of AI transforming the world.

1. Enhanced Decision Making:

AI can examine massive amounts of data and predict based on the analyzed data. However, AI provides better predictions than humans may have been able to identify in their research. Albert Einstein wrote that "The explanation of being a genius is making the complex simple." Nevertheless, Artificial Intelligence has become valuable in making significant decisions for complex businesses, giving those leveraging the AI model an edge over others that don't. In the health sector, AI provides patient data to recognize possible health threats and inform treatment plans as needed.

2. Personalization:

One of the essential benefits of AI is the proficiency to give unique experiences to users. Edureka noted in one of their articles that "Research from McKinsey found that companies excelling at personalization provide five to eight times the marketing ROI and increase their sales revenue by 10% over brands that do not. As much as personalization is stressful and overwhelming, it gives companies an edge over others who don't. Personalized messages and interactions build healthier customer relationships." Artificial intelligence has made it easy for companies to personalize messages to their target audience, helping them build stronger relationships with clients, increase productivity, and generate more sales for the organization.

3. Solving Complex Problems:

AI can solve challenges that are too hard for humans to solve alone. AI also helps in testing different theories to create new solutions to problems. AI helps humans quickly process large amounts of data and independently determine procedures they might not have seen. The inception of AI has helped several industries provide solutions to complex problems such as fraud, health challenges, weather forecasting, etc.

4. Better Risk Management:

AI can efficiently detect abnormalities, identify patterns, and scrutinize trends, making it an essential tool in risk management. Businesses can see patterns humans could easily overlook by analyzing large amounts of data. This can help companies identify and mitigate risks early on, potentially saving them millions in damages.

Industries in which AI is Widely Used:

Healthcare:

Artificial Intelligence helps doctors and other medical experts make more accurate diagnoses faster. The applications of AI used in healthcare create advanced machines that can detect ailments, recognize cancer cells, and solve other health problems. Implementing AI and a variety of medical historical data could lead to the discovery and creation of new drugs.

Creatives:

Artificial Intelligence aids creatives such as artists, content creators, musicians, and writers in their creative process. AI helps in the generation of new ideas, analyzing existing works, and improving the quality of creative work. AI can also help create contemporary art, music, and literature by analyzing existing outcomes and generating new variations.

Education:

Artificial Intelligence has made education easier for students and teachers in their learning and teaching processes. Using AI, the productivity level of an average student could increase among faculties and help them concentrate more. AI models can specify student learning styles and procedures, adapting to their own pace of learning. Video conferencing, audio summaries, textbooks, and materials can be made using artificial intelligence, creating a lasting experience for students without direct teacher involvement.

Transportation:

Modern means of transportation have become part and parcel of humans' daily lives in recent years through Artificial Intelligence. AI systems have improved traffic regulations, preventing road congestion and helping track road networks. Companies like Uber leverage the impact of AI to enhance communication, chatting, and decision-making among riders and customer services. Cargo logistics companies use AI for easy transport of goods, reducing delivery costs and improving asset management and operations.

Social Media Marketing:

AI aids with social media marketing by conforming to the audience's tone and approach. It can operate several tasks like ads performance, campaign reports, and increased post engagement. The use of AI differs on every social media platform, improving customer engagement for brands using social media for audience engagement and brand building.

Profound Text helps people understand conversations better and automatically translates different languages on Facebook. No matter your language in any part of the world, you can read and access other languages through the app, enhancing marketing strategies and increasing sales revenue. Twitter uses AI majorly for fraud detection and removing malicious content. Twitter also uses AI to suggest what kind of content you may like. However, you may want to engage in. Instagram uses AI to see the kind of content you love. These are just a few ways AI influences human lives, behavior, and lifestyle. It is a transformative technology that intensifies human abilities and will continue to play an essential function in transforming the world. As businesses and individuals continue to embrace the use of AI, we expect it to provide more inventive solutions to the challenges we face today. Conclusively, we must learn to approach the AI model's implementation responsibly to ensure its benefits are known and fully utilized while minimizing possible threats.

CHAPTER 2: WHAT ARE MACHINE LEARNING, ALGORITHMS, AND PROMPTS?

Machine learning has evolved into a powerful AI tool within the tech industry, demonstrating proficiency in analyzing extensive databases and generating predictions based on patterns. To fully grasp the concept of machine learning, it's essential to comprehend the roles of algorithms and prompts.

Machine learning, algorithms, and prompts share a close relationship, serving as crucial factors in data science to decipher large datasets and facilitate significant decision-making for individuals and businesses. According to Indeed.com, machine learning is where computers autonomously learn from data, closely tied to artificial intelligence, enabling devices to learn independently, detect patterns, make predictions, and analyze data.

Widely applied in diverse fields—from medical diagnosis to enhancing education quality, detecting fraud in financial transactions, to improving overall quality of life—machine learning relies on algorithms. Merriam-Webster defines algorithms as specific methods for solving problems, acting as sets of instructions guiding computers through various tasks. Algorithms serve as the core of machine learning, enabling computers to process and analyze vast amounts of data.

In our daily lives, algorithms manifest in activities like following a food recipe—a series of steps representing an algorithm to achieve a desired outcome. Categorizing objects, foods, and daily tasks also align with algorithmic principles, breaking down complex problems into manageable components for better understanding.

Another integral aspect of machine learning is the prompt, which assigns explicit tasks to the machine, facilitating learning and decision-making based on provided data. Prompts play a vital role in natural language processing, enhancing both personal and business aspects of human lives.

Prompts find application in various scenarios, such as chatbots and recommendation systems. For example, a chatbot may prompt users to provide names or addresses during a customer interaction. According to Wikipedia, prompt engineering involves transforming duties into a quick dataset, applying language standards in what's known as "prompt-based learning."

Machine learning's strength lies in its ability to improve rapidly. As more data is analyzed, and prompts are provided, algorithms can refine predictions, becoming more precise over time. These algorithms identify patterns, organizing them into different classes, enabling recognition of specific objects and faces, crucial for security measures and developmental analysis.

Shawn Harris emphasizes that machine learning influences the cost of prediction, embedded in all corporate decisions. Through accurate predictions, entrepreneurs can fundamentally alter operational processes, aiding companies in scaling efficiently.

Machine learning spans various industries, from finance and healthcare to retail and marketing. In finance, it analyzes market trends and predicts stock prices; in healthcare, it assesses medical records, identifying potential health risks. For retail and marketing, it delves into consumer behavior, recommending products or services. Additionally, machine learning, algorithms, and prompts play a pivotal role in search engine optimization through keyword analysis, assisting businesses in selecting the right keywords for websites.

These elements—machine learning, algorithms, and prompts—are integral parts of artificial intelligence, transforming diverse businesses and enhancing overall quality of life.

About Deep Learning

Deep learning, a subset of machine learning, represents a sophisticated approach to understanding and interpreting intricate patterns within vast datasets. As we delve into this realm, it's crucial to maintain the same narrative style while exploring the intricacies of deep learning.

Deep learning, often referred to as deep neural networks, stands at the forefront of technological innovation. Its distinctive feature lies in the utilization of artificial neural networks with multiple layers, enabling the model to comprehend complex representations of data. This layered structure mirrors the human brain's intricate connectivity, enhancing the system's ability to learn hierarchical features.

At its core, deep learning excels in automating feature extraction—a process vital for recognizing patterns and making informed decisions. The depth of these neural networks empowers the system to discern intricate details, making it adept at tasks such as image and speech recognition, natural language processing, and even autonomous decision-making.

A fundamental aspect of deep learning is the neural network, a computational model inspired by the human brain's neural structure. Each layer in the network processes specific features, progressively extracting higher-level representations as information traverses through the layers. This hierarchical learning mimics the human brain's cognitive processes, allowing the model to understand abstract concepts.

Convolutional Neural Networks (CNNs) and Recurrent Neural Networks (RNNs) are popular architectures within deep learning. CNNs excel in image recognition tasks by employing convolutional layers to extract spatial hierarchies, while RNNs shine in sequential data analysis, making them ideal for tasks like natural language processing and time series prediction.

The power of deep learning lies in its ability to automatically learn intricate features from raw data, eliminating the need for manual feature engineering. This capability significantly accelerates the model development process, making deep learning particularly advantageous in domains with large and complex datasets.

One notable application of deep learning is in autonomous vehicles, where the technology analyzes vast amounts of data from sensors and cameras to make real-time decisions. The ability to discern complex patterns in data allows these vehicles to navigate and respond to dynamic environments.

Moreover, deep learning plays a pivotal role in the field of healthcare, contributing to medical image analysis, disease diagnosis, and drug discovery. Its capacity to analyze and interpret complex medical data enhances diagnostic accuracy and aids in the development of innovative treatments.

Despite its remarkable capabilities, deep learning is not without challenges. The need for substantial computational resources and large datasets for training can pose barriers. Additionally, interpretability remains a concern, as the inner workings of complex neural networks often appear as 'black boxes.'

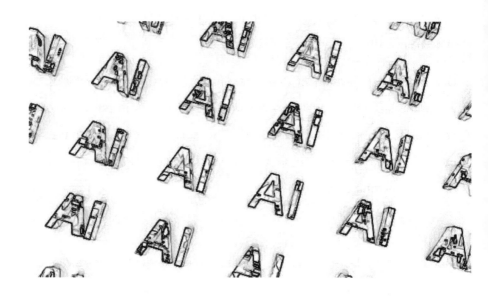

CHAPTER 3: AI IN HEALTHCARE, FINANCE, TRANSPORTATION, MANUFACTURING, ESPECIALLY RETAILING MARKETING.

In Chapter One, I explicitly explained the role of Artificial Intelligence (AI) and its impact on various industries. The implementation of AI models and tools has significantly increased the accuracy, efficiency, and momentum of business system operations worldwide. In this chapter, I will delve into how AI has profoundly impacted healthcare, finance, transportation, manufacturing, and retail marketing.

According to Grand View Research, the global demand for Artificial Intelligence (AI) was valued at U.S. $93.5 billion in 2021. From 2022 to 2030, the market is expected to thrive at a compound annual growth rate (CAGR) of 38.1%. As Tony Zapsnta noted on Microsourcing, this development can be largely attributed to the incessant analysis and innovation required by tech giants navigating the adoption of advanced technologies in various industries such as automobile, medicine, retail, finance, and manufacturing.

The efficiency of AI is a crucial aspect to consider. AI has been instrumental in automating businesses, providing support, and giving a competitive advantage to industries that leverage emerging trends and possibilities others may have overlooked.

Healthcare

AI has instigated lasting change in the healthcare industry, enhancing patient care, diagnosis, and medicine provision. It fosters communication among doctors and patients, facilitates drug expansion, and supports remote patient care. AI medical devices, including wearable detectors and home monitoring systems, enable doctors to track patient health data, provide treatment feedback, and automate tasks such as data entry and appointment scheduling. This not only allows medical professionals to focus on patient care but also minimizes human errors by providing quick ways to examine health histories, test results, and claims processing. AI medical devices are pivotal in detecting early signs of health issues, enabling timely intervention.

Banking And Finance

The finance industry has witnessed transformative changes with the development of AI-based apps and services. These applications have made banking more customer-friendly and relevant. AI aids in expense reduction, improving productivity and facilitating significant decisions based on the information provided by AI-based systems. In daily transactions, people demand enhanced fraud detection efforts from banks to secure customer history and finances. AI plays a crucial role in cybersecurity, enhancing online finance safety, identifying errors in schemes, and minimizing risks. With AI systems, banks can easily detect default activities and promptly alert customers.

Customer Experience

The implementation of AI systems has revolutionized customer experiences in the banking sector. Customers can easily access services and have a better experience, such as opening bank accounts from their homes and obtaining solutions to problems through calls and email messages. AI assists in obtaining client information promptly, ensuring outstanding customer experiences. AI also helps manage risks by assessing the likelihood of a consumer defaulting on a loan, predicting future behavior based on historical patterns.

Transportation

The transportation industry has significantly benefited from the impact of AI-powered systems, particularly in inferences and logistics management. AI contributes to the safety and cost-effectiveness of self-driving cars and trucks. Data analytics, as highlighted by Zesium in their blog, enhances transportation planning, increases safety, and improves overall logistics. Airlines leverage AI-powered systems to enhance flight schedules, reduce delays, and improve customer service. AI's influence has extended to reducing the stress of booking flights and accommodations through AI assistants and chatbots, allowing travelers to secure arrangements conveniently from their homes.

For the continuation of the chapter, please let me know if you'd like me to proceed.

Manufacturing

AI is reshaping the manufacturing sector by automating processes and enhancing efficiency. Intelligent manufacturers deploy AI-powered robots and sensors to streamline production, optimize supply chain management, and monitor the quantity and quality of goods. This automation reduces costs, improves product quality, and increases output. AI-powered sensors are utilized to supervise supplies and equipment, predicting maintenance needs and saving money. The speed of production is heightened as AI systems enable automatic task execution, meeting customer needs efficiently. Manufacturers benefit from AI's ability to address unforeseen challenges, maintain optimal decision-making, and increase overall efficiency in production processes.

Retailing

The retailing business has undergone a substantial transformation, moving beyond traditional channels and physical stores. With the rise of e-commerce, retailers are leveraging AI to automate operations and in-store strategies. Physical stores integrate AI-powered devices for cashier-less payments, goods monitoring, and digital displays, enhancing visibility and increasing sales revenue. Chatbots play a crucial role in interactive conversations with customers, responding to inquiries, offering product guidance, and resolving complaints. Retailers use AI to forecast product demand by analyzing prior sales, topography, buying trends, and other factors. AI oversees all aspects of the retail supply chain in real-time, including distribution, delivery, personnel, and inventory. Retailers can optimize pricing strategies with AI, assessing the effectiveness of different models to determine fair prices for their goods.

AI's application in retailing has not only improved customer shopping experiences but has also increased efficiency and profitability. The industry has adapted to changing customer behaviors and preferences, embracing AI to stay competitive.

Artificial Intelligence is now pervasive across various industries, playing a crucial role in streamlining operations and minimizing expenditures associated with tedious tasks. As AI tools continue to evolve, industries are utilizing these systems to train their employees, optimizing human capital for optimal results.

CHAPTER 4: THE BENEFIT OF AI IN REAL ESTATE, BUY AND SELL, RENT, ADVERTISING

AI has transcended human socialization, home management, and tech-related fields, making its mark in almost every business, including real estate. The transformative power of AI in real estate management is evident, significantly benefiting processes like buying, selling, advertising, and showcasing properties efficiently.

Human errors in real estate transactions can result in significant consequences. For instance, a sales representative recording inadequate transactions may pose considerable challenges. While one could learn about these errors early on, they might still lead to unfortunate events. AI plays a crucial role in mitigating human error by ensuring accurate data entry. The system remains energized as long as it is adequately trained, consistently getting things right.

AI model systems excel in producing diverse pricing strategies, utilizing trends and data to establish reasonable property prices. Real Estate apps employing AI streamline the process of finding the perfect buyer, making it faster and more efficient. Landlords benefit from AI systems that provide access to tenants' relevant data, transactions, essential documentation, and other valuable resources.

Furthermore, marketing campaigns for real estate businesses can be executed through AI-generated text systems. These systems generate tailored programs that resonate with the target audience, offering the convenience of buyers exploring properties remotely without the need for physical visits.

Virtual technologies enable property exploration from anywhere in the world, eliminating the necessity of entering the country. This remote exploration provides a comprehensive understanding of the property being considered for purchase without physical presence, facilitating high-speed negotiations.

ChatGPT emerges as a valuable tool for realtors in marketing analysis. Traditionally, market analysis involves navigating various sources like County Tax Records, Zillow, and MLS. ChatGPT streamlines these sources into a single platform, presenting comprehensive data on one page, expediting the entire process. However, caution is advised regarding the information it produces, as some may require updating.

Additionally, ChatGPT aids in efficient property management, relieving realtors of administrative tasks. It enhances professionalism in AI, assisting in email composition and communication with prospects or clients, ultimately increasing efficiency. ChatGPT's capabilities extend to handling tenant-related questions and communication, exemplified by inputting statements like, "Write me a 30-day quick payment notice to a tenant who is three months behind on rent."

Check this out.

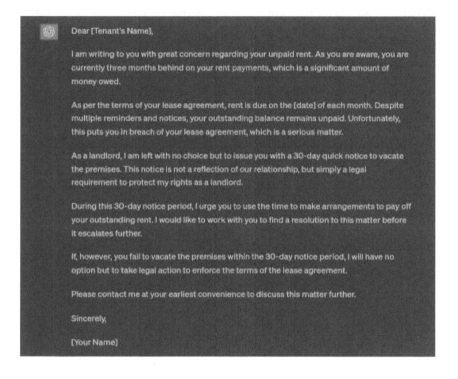

Dear [Tenant's Name],

I am writing to you with great concern regarding your unpaid rent. As you are aware, you are currently three months behind on your rent payments, which is a significant amount of money owed.

As per the terms of your lease agreement, rent is due on the [date] of each month. Despite multiple reminders and notices, your outstanding balance remains unpaid. Unfortunately, this puts you in breach of your lease agreement, which is a serious matter.

As a landlord, I am left with no choice but to issue you with a 30-day quick notice to vacate the premises. This notice is not a reflection of our relationship, but simply a legal requirement to protect my rights as a landlord.

During this 30-day notice period, I urge you to use the time to make arrangements to pay off your outstanding rent. I would like to work with you to find a resolution to this matter before it escalates further.

If, however, you fail to vacate the premises within the 30-day notice period, I will have no option but to take legal action to enforce the terms of the lease agreement.

Please contact me at your earliest convenience to discuss this matter further.

Sincerely,

[Your Name]

That is precisely what I needed to see. Your request must be specific to receive an accurate response to any command you input. Feel free to go ahead and try it out.

Additionally, as a real estate agent, effective communication between you and your tenants is crucial. For instance, if you intend to raise the rent due to various factors, conveying this sensitive information must be done in a manner that is professional and respectful. With the assistance of ChatGPT, you can generate a well-detailed, personalized letter explaining why the rent needs to increase, among other details.

ChatGPT can also assist you in crafting the perfect description for a house you want to sell as a realtor. For example, suppose you aim to sell a three-bedroom apartment with a square-foot home featuring a recently renovated kitchen and basement, along with a double garage in the back. With this information, you can obtain a compelling description of the house; all you need to do is input the accurate details into the app.

Feel free to check this out too.

Welcome to your dream home! This stunning three-bedroom apartment offers the perfect combination of style, comfort, and convenience. With a spacious square foot layout, you'll have plenty of room to spread out and enjoy your new home.

One of the standout features of this apartment is the recently renovated kitchen. With brand new appliances, sleek countertops, and modern finishes, you'll be cooking up a storm in no time. The open layout of the kitchen and living area makes it the perfect space for entertaining guests or enjoying quality time with family.

But that's not all - this apartment also boasts a fully finished basement, providing even more space for a home office, gym, or additional living area. And if you're in need of some extra storage space, the double garage in the back of the property is the perfect solution.

With three spacious bedrooms, this apartment is the perfect place to call home. Whether you're looking to create a cozy retreat or a stylish oasis, there's plenty of room to make this space your own.

Located in a desirable neighborhood, this apartment offers easy access to all the amenities you could want, from shops and restaurants to parks and schools. Don't miss out on this amazing opportunity to own your dream home - schedule a viewing today!

CChatGPT can help answer all your budding questions about real estate and provide the necessary information for your real estate business. The question is, how can ChatGPT assist in generating sales and revenue in the real estate industry?

It's known that the real estate business is a profitable niche that offers countless opportunities to yield significant Return on Investment (ROI). To thrive in this business, investors must have reliable sources of information to analyze the market, as mentioned earlier, and make accurate decisions. This is where the ChatGPT system can play a vital role in assisting investors in obtaining the correct information to boost sales.

One significant advantage of using ChatGPT to make money is through property research. ChatGPT can save investors the stress of searching for properties that meet their financial and investment goals. Additionally, ChatGPT can be used to search for properties that match specific criteria. Investors can specify the type of property they want, the location, and other factors.

ChatGPT can also be used to provide customer service to buyers and sellers. It can answer common questions about properties, buying and selling, generate social media posts, and cover other related subjects. This can help investors offer better customer service and enhance their reputation in the market.

ChatGPT can also help create compelling copy for your real estate business. This is explicitly crafted to meet your target audience and marketing objectives, aiming to generate more sales for your business. You can leverage Chat GPT's copywriting skills for your business, including email campaigns, direct mail letters, and website copy.

ChatGPT can also provide predictive analytics by examining historical data to predict future market trends. This information can enable investors to make strategic decisions about buying and selling properties, helping them stay ahead of the curve in a rapidly changing market.

Chat GPT is an effective system to help real estate investors make money by renting out properties. Through the use of this system, it can generate property information, automate responses to prospects' most frequently asked questions and challenges, and discuss rental processes and prices with them.

It can automate different parts of the rental process, such as scheduling property viewings, processing rental applications, and handling other related processes. This saves you much time and effort as a real estate investor, allowing you to focus on different aspects of your business, such as maintenance and proper management.

Another usefulness of utilizing ChatGPT in real estate is correctly processing large amounts of data. It explicitly describes the properties, such as size, location, amenities, and rates—valuable information prospects are eager to know when finding a rental property quickly while considering other options suitable for their convenience.

ChatGPT can also help in retaining these tenants. Gathering data about these tenants, such as their preferences and history, will help investors create personalized interaction strategies to keep them engaged. All these processes will boost the possibility of long-term rental income.

Additionally, ChatGPT can assist you as a real estate investor in attracting a broader range of potential tenants, leading to a demand for rental properties and higher rental rates. Once their demographics and interests are known, real estate agents can generate effective marketing campaigns.

Another way that ChatGPT can produce money in the real estate industry is through advertising. Real estate advertising is essential as it helps brokers market their properties to potential customers and residents. With ChatGPT's processing capacities, it can be used to create content and marketing strategies that will focus on the target audience.

ChatGPT studies consumer behavior and preferences, investigating ways in which buyers behave and determining the most persuasive marketing methods. For instance, ChatGPT can explore the online search behavior of prospects and tenants to determine the keywords they use to search for properties. This data can be used to develop targeted promotion campaigns that use these keywords to attract the attention of potential buyers and renters.

Virtual assistants can also provide personalized suggestions to customers based on what they like, want, or need.

Another way ChatGPT can help through advertising is the usage of Chatbots for lead generation. ChatGPT can be integrated into a real estate website or social media page as a chatbot. These Chatbots can ask customers questions, generate input about available properties, and plan meetings with brokers. You can get more leads by creating this kind of model as a real estate agent.

ChatGPT can also be incorporated into the Show Housing System. Show Housing is a platform that helps real estate agents and brokers show their properties to potential buyers. Using ChatGPT, Show Housing makes buying and selling more efficient using technology and data. The platform has a database of properties, and users can search for properties based on their preferences.

The Show Housing System, using ChatGPT, makes buying and selling more efficient through the utilization of technology and data. The platform boasts a database of properties, allowing users to search for properties based on their preferences.

This seamless integration of ChatGPT in the real estate industry extends to advertising strategies. Real estate advertising is essential for helping brokers market their properties to potential customers and residents. Leveraging ChatGPT's processing capacities, it can be utilized to craft content and marketing strategies that specifically target the desired audience.

ChatGPT not only studies consumer behavior and preferences but also delves into understanding how buyers behave, enabling the identification of the most effective marketing methods. For example, ChatGPT can analyze the online search behavior of prospects and tenants, determining the keywords they use to search for properties. This valuable data can then be employed to develop targeted promotional campaigns, incorporating these keywords to attract the attention of potential buyers and renters.

Virtual assistants, powered by ChatGPT, offer an additional layer of personalized support to customers based on their preferences and needs. This capability enhances the overall customer experience, making interactions more tailored and engaging.

Another significant avenue where ChatGPT contributes to the real estate industry's financial success is through the utilization of Chatbots for lead generation. By integrating ChatGPT into a real estate website or social media page as a chatbot, these automated systems can engage customers, gather information about available properties, and schedule meetings with brokers. This innovative approach can significantly boost lead generation for real estate agents.

In summary, ChatGPT emerges as a multifaceted tool for real estate professionals. From assisting in property research, providing customer service, and crafting compelling copy, to offering predictive analytics and enhancing advertising strategies, ChatGPT's capabilities extend across various facets of the real estate business. Its integration into systems like Show Housing and utilization in lead-generating Chatbots further exemplify its potential in revolutionizing how the real estate industry operates and generates income.

CHAPTER 5: WHAT IS CHATGPT, WHAT IS CHAT GPT3, AND CHAT GPT4

ChatGPT, or GPT-3, is a practical language model invented and created by OpenAI. It is based on the GPT-3.5 architecture, which allows it to execute a vast array of natural language processing tasks, including translation, text generation, summarization, and other complex tasks. The tool has limitations at present, but with time, it will improve further. ChatGPT was released for public use on the 30th of November, 2022; since its inception, it has been trending.

ChatGPT is skilled in answering complex questions, creating and curating strategic ideas in any niche, and developing chatbots, making it an exceptional tool for various applications, including game development, creative writing, and more. ChatGPT is a machine learning model trained on tremendous text data. This training allows it to understand the nuances and intricacies of natural language, enabling it to yield answers to multiple questions simultaneously.

One of the most crucial features is its ability to generate personalized responses to various queries. Through unsupervised learning, it can develop different answers at once. This design makes it highly well-suited for processing natural language text, allowing it to generate high-quality answers ideally and faster.

In the area of programming, ChatGPT has pre-established codes designed to perform numerous tasks. Chatbots can be used to organize conferences and seminars, provide advanced search functionality, and handle various other tasks. The programmers continually update the command catalog, enhancing its programmability and multi-functionality.

Another tremendous functionality is that ChatGPT is available 24 hours a day to respond to human needs and wants promptly. As explained in previous chapters, chatbots make it easier for both customers and sales representatives, avoiding clients' prolonged waits for their requests.

ChatGPT aids in scalability, enabling the development of performance assessments, expansion strategies, and analysis plans, equipping organizations with better, objective, and data-driven methods for performance management.

In the monetary aspect, ChatGPT can be infused in all business sectors to generate more funds. For instance, Affiliate Marketers make use of ChatGPT to promote other companies. Brands generate unique links for individuals interested in affiliating their products or services. These links lead people to where they can purchase the goods, allowing marketers to earn a percentage commission for every sale made through them.

With ChatGPT, you can create more content to reach out to the target audience that needs the product while generating income. As an Online

Creator struggling to write scripts, ChatGPT can simplify the process by generating content that you can edit to your tone and style. Utilize all apps to edit it into voiceovers and compelling videos for your brand. Through that, you can monetize your work, making it easier if you aim to become a YouTuber.

Online content creators face challenges with drama and controversy as they become more popular. Fans and haters may harass them in real life. Fellow content creators may taunt them to elicit outrage and create accessible content. This is why some people create online personas, using a different character and name to separate online work from the real world.

ChatGPT makes this method more accessible by writing your script. Then, edit it to reflect your style, feed it to an AI voiceover app, and embed the AI voice into your videos. Eventually, you may earn ad revenue from your videos, making it easier to start your YouTube career.

You can also offer ChatGPT as a service to individuals and industries requiring natural language processing capabilities. This can be done through applications, programming languages, or other integrations, with enterprises paying for the service on a subscription basis.

ChatGPT-4, on the other hand, is the latest improvement in the AI enterprise. It is similar to ChatGPT Pro, based on the GPT-3.5

architecture. It is also an AI-based conversational mechanism using natural language processing to meet the needs of humans and answer their questions, just like ChatGPT. ChatGPT-4 was developed based on GPT-3, an AI model that has revolutionized the field of natural language processing.

ChatGPT-4 is an advanced technology integrated with developed abilities such as contingent knowledge and personalization. One crucial characteristic of ChatGPT-4 is its capacity to immerse in human discussions compared to ChatGPT-4. The system has been coached on an extensive exhibition of language data, enabling it to comprehend and imitate human speech habits and idioms. ChatGPT-4 can carry on a conversation that makes you feel you are talking to a human being.

Another impressive characteristic of ChatGPT-4 is that it can understand different contexts and provide responses that apply to your position or situation. For instance, if you ask ChatGPT-4 for directions to somewhere you haven't been, it can provide a beneficial response, including a map and directions. Also, if you ask ChatGPT to tell you something specific about a particular place, it gives a more detailed and precise answer compared to GPT-3. ChatGPT-4 is faster, more precise, and more detailed, increasing the response time and optimizing its ability to process and respond to questions.

GPT-4 has an incredible capacity to differentiate and induce diverse dialects; it can comprehend and respond quickly according to the tone of the user. This makes the AI model more subjective and natural. GPT-4 can translate words into different languages according to other cultures, provinces, and dialects. Differentiating dialects can be complicated because each one has its pronunciation, vocabulary, and unique grammar. All these may be lacking in the standard language model. GPT-4 can help give the proper common mod and create precise wordings, even if pronounced differently.

ChatGPT focuses mainly on texts, but GPT-4 can comment on and analyze images and graphics. It can transcribe content shown through an image, analyze trends in graphs, and create information in numerous photos. This benefits content creators and educators due to its accuracy and quick results. GPT-4 can solve complicated problems, even mathematical and scientific ones, going beyond the capabilities of GPT-3.5. This is undoubtedly one of the significant benefits of Chat GPT-4. The language model can solve advanced calculus problems and simulate chemical reactions.

GPT-4 has enhanced immensely, with better comprehension of scientific processes and mathematical concepts. Its mathematical skills involve solving geometry operations, complex additional algebra, and physics. The modeling ability and language allow you to analyze challenging scientific texts. There are several ways you can make money through GPT-4. You can build websites and landing pages for yourself and other businesses. Turn your creative idea into an app or website through GPT-4, helping several companies create opportunities and allowing many start-ups to thrive quickly in the market.

Another unique way to make money from GPT-4 is by writing and selling digital products. Create a simple and exciting topic or material that compels your audience to buy through the help of ChatGPT-4. It can transform your knowledge into fast-selling digital products, regardless of your position in the field. GPT-4 can make your blogging journey easier, helping you write content for yourself in less time. It is an excellent tool for transcribing videos and audio through the machine-learning model, allowing you to add transcription services to your portfolio and provide services on freelance platforms.

Additionally, you can use GPT-4 to translate materials and products into other languages, delivering quick and accurate translation services to individuals globally, supporting your communication skills. Through these various applications, GPT-4 demonstrates its versatility and potential in contributing to multiple fields and business sectors. The AI model continues to evolve, offering innovative solutions and opportunities for individuals and organizations alike.

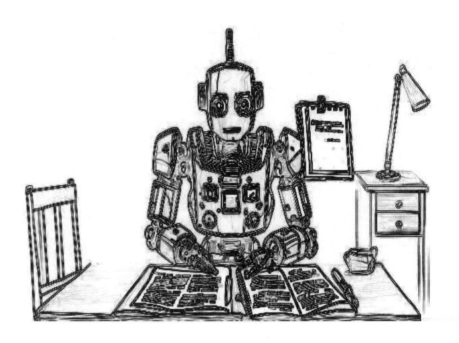

CHAPTER 6: BUILDING A BUSINESS MODEL WITH CHATGPT: START-UP AND BUSINESS EVOLUTION

Over time, businesses have undergone substantial adaptations and transformations owing to technological advances, changes in customer behavior, and globalization. The first stage of business evolution started with the industrial revolution. The innovation of machines and devices with different manufacturing techniques has led to the creation of other products and services on a vast scale, producing production in massive numbers. At the same time, they are being sold at low cost. Low prices result in higher demand for goods, which results in profits for several businesses.

The second stage of business evolution started with the rise of marketing and prioritizing consumer delight. From the innovation of machines, businesses focus on creating products that satisfy the wants and needs of consumers. However, marketing became necessary for creating awareness and bringing in sales. Business owners realize the expansion of sales and marketing promotions.

Businesses take a massive turn through expanded evolution. The rise of the internet and digital technology changed how business owners run their businesses. Local businesses were able to attain a global audience and build multinational companies. Several new business strategies, like mobile marketing, social media marketing, e-commerce, and many more, rose through the internet. Through data analytics, businesses get to understand consumer behavior and expand targeted marketing systems and techniques.

As business evolves, customers want more than buying products and services. They want an extraordinary experience when using your product and services. Companies that use personalized messages sell more than those that don't. With the rise of ChatGPT, virtual reality, chatbots, and artificial intelligence, businesses can now produce more fascinating and engaging content and experience for their customers.

Businesses have evolved through technological advancements and changes in consumer behavior. ChatGPT has been incorporated into business systems. However, it has been disrupted. The future of business evolution will likely be shaped by technological advances and consumer behavior changes. One trend likely to continue is the focus on customer experience, as consumers become more demanding and discerning. Businesses that can create a personalized and seamless experience across multiple touchpoints will be more successful in the future. These models create better opportunities for entrepreneurs and organizations.

In previous chapters, I discussed how ChatGPT can be incorporated into several business sectors. ChatGPT has gone beyond asking random questions for people to helping grow a successful brand both on the Internet and physically.

In this chapter, you will learn how to build a successful business model using ChatGPT, especially as a startup. Let's dive into it. Here are five things you need to know as a startup who wants to use ChatGPT to grow a successful business.

1. You need to understand the potential of ChatGPT. This language model helps businesses and individuals generate human-like text responses as quickly as possible, given a prompt or a command. ChatGPT is taught and tweaked to comprehend and answer precise disciplines, making it a powerful mechanism for different businesses and enterprises. The capability application of this language model in the industry comprises lead generation, content creation, personalized messages and recommendations, customer services and support, and several other influential roles. By harnessing the ability of ChatGPT, industries can automate repetitious duties, give fast and valid answers to customer queries, and provide personalized understanding to your business.

2. There are likely limited resources for start-up businesses. However, we need to focus on building a solid customer base. Enforcing the language model ChatGPT into their social media platforms, websites, and other platforms that people can reach

out to them will go a long way. ChatGPT provides 24/7 customer support without necessarily having an extensive support system team. ChatGPT can help you regulate customers' common questions, provide product information, and solve fundamental challenges. This will enhance customer delight in your organization and relieve your company's stress while you focus on other activities.

3. As your business grows as a start-up, you can expand ChatGPT functions' benefit. You can leverage ChatGPT to generate leads and drive sales for your business by teaching the language model on recorded customer data and information. The model can help you identify your customers' purchase behaviors, patterns, and preferences. This can help you create personalized products for your target audience, develop s targeted marketing campaigns, and engage customers in meaningful conversations via your platform to increase the conversion rate of your business.

4. In the maturity stage of your business, you can use ChatGPT to increase internal processes and enhance your company's efficiency. ChatGPT can help you with predictive analytics of your business, optimize your supply chain, and manage your goods and supply by analyzing market trends and historical data. The model provides helpful insights for sound decision-

making. owever, ChatGPT can be incorporated with project management tools, which enables different teams to partner more effectively and facilitates the smooth running of the organization. ChatGPT can help you customize your audience and your business's unique needs.

5. As industries develop, they may have outstanding prerequisites beyond what ChatGPT can do. Fortunately, ChatGPT can be upgraded to meet the business's distinct needs by training the system on proprietary data and inducing domain-specific knowledge. You can create chatbots that align perfectly with your business tone, brand voice, vision and mission statements, customer expectations, etc. This ensures an accurate and humanly personalized experience with the customer. However, it skyrockets the business and sets it apart from those doing almost the same company as you. Additionally, being transparent with customers about their interactions with a chatbot and getting human escalation options whenever needed is crucial. Information and data privacy of your customers must be taken seriously.

CHAPTER 7: STEP-BY-STEP GUIDE TO ACCESS AND UTILIZE ALL THE POWER OF CHATGPT

In this chapter, I will guide you through the process of using ChatGPT to answer any question of your choice and building your application on this language model. Let's dive into it.

Step 1: Select the Suitable Medium

The initial phase of accessing the language model, ChatGPT, involves choosing the suitable medium. You can access ChatGPT through different platforms, such as OpenAI's API, Hugging Face's Transformer, and GPT-3 playground. OpenAI's API offers outstanding features, but a subscription is required before access. Hugging Face's Transformers, a Python library, provides access to ChatGPT and other AI-powered language models. GPT-3 Playground is an unrestricted platform allowing interaction with ChatGPT in a browser-based environment like Chrome.

Step 2: Create Your Account

Once you've identified the preferred platform, you only need to set up the account. For OpenAI's API, you must subscribe and create an API key. GPT-3 Playground and Hugging Face's Transformers do not require a sign-up process, but you may need to install necessary dependencies using the Python library.

Step 3: Interact with ChatGPT

After setting up your account, you can start interacting with ChatGPT. The language model is versatile, handling tasks such as generating text, summarizing, and answering questions. To use ChatGPT, provide it with a command by typing short text commands for your desired results. For example, if you want ChatGPT to write about a Gucci Bag, your command could be "Write me 100 words about a Gucci Bag." ChatGPT will respond based on your instructions.

Step 4: Edit The Outcome

ChatGPT, being an advanced language model, may produce responses that need refinement. To enhance results, you might need to edit the output to your taste or adjust it based on feedback. For instance, if ChatGPT provides an inadequate solution, you can use the "thumbs up" or "thumbs down" icon. Clicking "thumbs down" prompts the model to generate a new answer based on your feedback.

Step 5: Experiment with Several Commands

To optimize your experience, experiment with different commands. For example, if you want ChatGPT to generate questions on Content

Marketing, type "Write me ten questions on Content Marketing." For starting a discussion on Artificial Intelligence, your command could be, "Let's start a discussion on Artificial Intelligence." Explore various commands for the best ChatGPT experience.

Here are the steps to follow in building an application; let's dive into it.

Step 1: Select a Platform That Is Convenient for You

Numerous platforms authorize access to ChatGPT, including Hugging Face's API, OpenAI's API, and EleutherAI's API. Each has its benefits and drawbacks. OpenAI's API is popular but requires an invitation and is costly. Hugging Face's API is cheaper but has lower performance than OpenAI. EleutherAI's API is an open-source option under development, potentially valuable in the future.

Step 2: Get Your API Key

Once you've chosen a platform, obtaining an API key is essential. This unique identifier grants access to the platform's resources. The process depends on the chosen forum, typically involving account creation and following platform instructions.

Step 3: Set Up Your Environment

Setting up your environment is crucial when using ChatGPT, involving installing necessary libraries and components on your computer. The prerequisites depend on your chosen platform, and most platforms provide documented, precise instructions on environment setup.

Step 4: Choose Your Preferred Model

ChatGPT offers various pre-trained models with different complexities and performances, ranging from small to giant models and task-specific models like language translation. The model size choice depends on your specific needs. Small models are faster but limited in function, while large models are more authentic but require more computational resources and have longer response times.

Step 5: Create Your Desired Application

For this step, specifics depend on your use case, but general procedures can guide you. Write code to send a request to the ChatGPT API, specifying the desired model and input text for response generation. The API will respond with an answer in JSON format, which you can analyze and display. Handle errors likely to occur during the request, such as timeouts and network errors. Edit the response from ChatGPT to enhance the model for a specific task or post-process the text to remove unwanted content.

Step 6: Test and Deploy Your Application

Once your application is ready, test it thoroughly. If satisfied, copy and paste it into your environment, configuring your API key, setting up your web server, and ensuring the application is safe and scalable.

Step 7: Monitor and Improve Your Application

Monitor your application for issues and continuously improve content and models. This ensures ongoing optimization and delivers the best experience to users.

CHAPTER 8: WEBSITE CREATION AND CONTENT WITH CHATGPT.

ChatGPT is an exceptional AI tool that can transform your work. With ChatGPT, you can create a website or portfolio for your businesses and services. In this chapter, I will walk you through creating your website with ChatGPT and how you can generate content for your website.

The first step you need to know is to identify why you want to create a website for your business before delving into the technological factors. Then, after identifying the basic needs of the website, type "ChatGPT" into your browser to either log into your existing account or create a new one. Enter your email address and phone number to make a new account. Then click on "Continue".

OpenAI will verify your account by sending a verification request through your email address. Once you click on the button, it will redirect you to the onboarding account page of OpenAI, where you will input your name and phone number. A verification code will be sent to your phone number either through SMS or WhatsApp.

After completing these steps, you will be directed to the ChatGPT interface, where you can use it directly. Before building your website with ChatGPT, you must acquire a domain name and subscribe to a hosting plan. A domain name is linked to an IP address on the Internet and authorizes people to find your website online. Hosting serves as storage where all your website files are stored. Ensure you pick a unique name by checking various websites to see if your chosen name has been taken. You can simply input "Domain Name Search" on Google to check it out.

Next, ask ChatGPT to provide an easy outline for your website tailored to your specific business. For instance, you can input "Write me a website outline for my clothing business of 3 pages." Here is the result I got from a simple text:

"Write me a Website outline for my clothing business of 3 pages.

ChatGPT

Sure! Here's a design for a 3-page website for your clothing business:

Page 1: Home

- Header Section

- Logo: Display your business logo prominently.

- Navigation Menu: Include links to other pages of the website, such as "Home," "Shop," "About Us," "Contact," etc.

- Hero Section

- Background Image: Feature an attractive image showcasing your clothing products.

- Catchy Tagline: Include a short and captivating tagline representing your brand.

- Featured Products Section

- Showcase a selection of your best-selling or newly released clothing items.

- Include high-quality product images, brief descriptions, and pricing.

- Add "Shop Now" buttons linking to the respective product pages.

- About Us Section

- Briefly introduce your clothing business, its mission, and values.

- Share your brand story and what sets you apart from competitors.

- Include any relevant credentials, awards, or partnerships.

- Customer Testimonials Section

- Highlight positive reviews or testimonials from satisfied customers.

- Include customer names, photos (with permission), and their feedback.

- Testimonials should emphasize quality, style, and customer satisfaction.

- Call-to-Action Section

- Encourage visitors to take action, such as signing up for newsletters or following your social media accounts.

- Include a compelling CTA button, e.g., "Subscribe Now" or "Follow Us."

- Footer Section

- Contact Information: Provide your business address, phone number, and email.

- Links: Include quick links to important pages, such as "Privacy Policy," "Terms and Conditions," etc.

Page 2: Shop

- Header and Navigation Menu

- Repeat the header and navigation menu from the home page.

- Product Categories

- List the different categories of clothing items you offer, such as "Men's Clothing," "Women's Clothing," "Accessories," etc.

- Include thumbnail images representing each category.

- Product Listings

- Display a grid or list of clothing products within the selected category.

- Include product images, names, prices, and a brief description.

- Add "Add to Cart" buttons for each product.

- Filtering and Sorting Options

- Provide filters to help visitors narrow their product search, such as size, color, price range, etc.

- Allow sorting options, such as "Price: Low to High" or "Newest Arrivals."

- Product Details

- Create individual product pages with detailed information for each item.

- Include multiple images, product descriptions, size charts, material information, etc.

- Add a prominent "Add to Cart" button and options to select the size, color, etc.

Page 3: About Us and Contact

- Header and Navigation Menu

- Repeat the header and navigation menu from the home page.

- About Us

- Provide a comprehensive overview of your clothing business.

- Include your brand's history, mission, values, and unique selling points.

- Share information about your team, designers, or manufacturing process.

- Contact Information

- Display your business address, phone number, and email.

- Offer a contact form for visitors to send inquiries or messages.

- Mention your customer support availability and response times.

- Social Media Integration

- Include icons and links to your social media profiles.

- Encourage visitors to follow you on platforms like Facebook, Instagram, Twitter, etc.

- Showcase your latest social media posts or testimonials from customers.

- Additional Information

- Add links to important pages, such as "Shipping Information," "Return Policy," etc.

This is great. With this, you can get an idea of your website's appearance. ChatGPT just gave a simple outline of how you can go about each page and some ideas you can input on each page. You can go ahead and try it out. However, ChatGPT can help you with your heading, unique selling point, and even your call to action. It would be best to edit it to your tone and style; you are good to go. ChatGPT can also help you with website themes and suggest how you can go about each piece. Then you can tell ChatGPT to create an HTML code with the number of pages you need to make the website. Your prompts could be: Create a homepage design. That includes the About Us, header section, home, shop, and contact. If you don't like exactly what it outputs, you can tweak your prompt by asking ChatGPT. Also, you might need a budding web developer handy or someone who can help you correct errors or unforeseen challenges. ChatGPT could stop halfway if the result is long. When that occurs, you can write 'Continue The Script.' Input the follow-up command to make ChatGPT start from where it stopped. ChatGPT can help you create other outlines you believe your website needs to have. You can also use ChatGPT to generate the CSS code or use already-made fonts. For example, you can use the existing WordPress templates and themes if you are building a WordPress website. In generating content for your website, ChatGPT can help you create tons of content for your website. It can also generate ideas on things you could post. For example, you could input this prompt for the website. "I just created a website for my clothing business. I need you to generate the best ideas for my brand, with specific content for my home page, about us page, and product page." Here is the prompt: ChatGPT can also help you find intriguing keyword ideas for SEO. Your command could be: Help me create SEO keywords for blog posts for my clothing store. However, this should include highly researched keywords but less competition. Then you can copy the results to search volume like Ahrefs to see results. ChatGPT can also help you craft compelling headlines and the body of your article. It can help create copy and content for your brand, including product descriptions and blog posts. You can input something like Write me a product description of a designer dress" or Create multiple compelling headlines I can use for a designer dress. With ChatGPT, you have a website ready with all the necessary information that needs to be included. Go try it out.

CHAPTER 9: MARKETING AND LEAD GENERATION WITH CHATGPT (USED TO GET CUSTOMER INFORMATION FOR SOCIAL MEDIA CAMPAIGNS)

In the previous chapters, you discovered one of the fantastic benefits of ChatGPT—it can generate quality leads for individuals and businesses, making it easier for several organizations. In this chapter, I'll delve into how you can leverage the ChatGPT language model to grow your brand or business.

Building on what we've discussed earlier, where brands and companies continually seek innovative ways to generate organic leads and attract buying customers, lead generation is crucial for nurturing prospects, clients, and customers to drive revenue growth and foster genuine customer interaction. Let's explore in-depth how ChatGPT can be a game-changer for your business.

One of the key advantages is its availability and the ability to address instant challenges in businesses. When incorporated into your website or chatbot, ChatGPT enables brands and companies to engage with leads at any time. Customers receive prompt responses, providing a great opportunity to convert these leads into potential customers.

Integrated into a website or chatbot, ChatGPT facilitates engagement with potential leads at any time, irrespective of time zones or working hours. This accessibility ensures immediate responses to queries, enhancing customer satisfaction and increasing the likelihood of converting leads into customers.

ChatGPT excels at analyzing the context and intent of user queries, delivering excellent answers and suggestions. It gathers relevant information from potential leads, such as their priorities, demands, and pain points, to offer targeted solutions or products. By doing so, ChatGPT enhances the user experience, strengthening the connection between the business and the prospect.

Moreover, ChatGPT assists in segmenting leads, attracting quality leads by asking essential questions and gathering vital information. Once a lead is generated, ChatGPT aids in sending automated messages, obtaining more information, and sharing related content from previous discussions. This automated lead nurturing not only saves time but ensures consistency.

As ChatGPT has evolved over time, it now analyzes large amounts of data to understand audience or customer preferences, enabling the development of successful lead conversion strategies. Continual optimization enhances ChatGPT's effectiveness in generating quality leads, aligning businesses with the right marketing strategies.

On another note, social media has emerged as an effective tool for connecting with businesses and promoting products and services through campaigns like ads and organic reach. Obtaining relevant customer information is crucial, and here ChatGPT plays a vital role in easing marketing stress and producing optimum results.

In utilizing ChatGPT for marketing campaigns, clarity and specificity in your purpose are paramount. Similar to creating websites and applications, knowing the exact goal of your social media campaign is essential. Craft specific questions to understand customer preferences and perceptions, and ChatGPT can generate engaging questions based on your input, providing a seamless customer experience.

Continuing with the utilization of ChatGPT, it can assist in generating content for running ads, stimulating audience participation, and obtaining testimonials. It can also serve as a virtual assistant incorporated into social media accounts, engaging users in personalized discussions and compelling them to share meaningful conversations.

Privacy and data security are critical considerations, and ChatGPT ensures that customer information remains safe. It has significantly eased the stress for new brands and business owners, providing optimized results without excessive spending on marketing. In the next chapter, I'll guide you on maximizing productivity using AI systems.

Continuing our exploration of ChatGPT's role in marketing and lead generation, let's delve further into how this powerful tool can revolutionize your business strategies.

As we've discussed, ChatGPT's integration into your website or chatbot offers unparalleled advantages, enabling instant engagement with potential leads regardless of time zones or working hours. This immediate responsiveness enhances customer satisfaction and significantly boosts the chances of converting leads into loyal customers.

An additional noteworthy feature of ChatGPT lies in its ability to analyze user queries' context and intent, providing not just responses but valuable insights. By collecting pertinent information from potential leads—such as their priorities, demands, and pain points—ChatGPT facilitates personalized and targeted interactions. This not only enriches the user experience but also deepens the connection between your business and its audience.

Moreover, ChatGPT's capacity to assist in segmenting leads is a valuable asset. By posing essential questions and extracting key information, it aids in attracting high-quality leads. Once leads are generated, ChatGPT doesn't stop there. It seamlessly handles automated lead nurturing—sending messages, gathering more information, and sharing relevant content from previous discussions. This not only saves time and effort but ensures consistency in your approach.

ChatGPT's evolution over time has been remarkable. Its ability to analyze vast amounts of data, understand audience preferences, and continually enhance lead conversion strategies positions it as a dynamic and effective tool in the marketing landscape. As ChatGPT adapts, it not only generates quality leads for businesses but also guides them in channeling their marketing strategies to the most effective avenues.

Shifting our focus to the realm of social media, an indispensable tool for businesses in the contemporary landscape, ChatGPT plays a pivotal role in alleviating marketing challenges and yielding optimal results. Here are some guidelines for utilizing ChatGPT in your social media campaigns:

1. Clarity of Purpose: Clearly define the purpose of your social media campaign. This echoes the advice provided in earlier chapters regarding creating websites and applications. Knowing why you're running an ad helps in obtaining relevant customer information.

2. Focused Questions: Craft meaningful and specific questions that align with your campaign goals. For instance, if you're launching a new product, inquire about people's perceptions and suggestions. Utilize open questions to encourage honest responses, and let ChatGPT assist in generating engaging queries tailored to your input, ensuring a seamless customer experience.

3. Content Generation for Ads: Leverage ChatGPT to generate content for your ads. Encourage your audience to share experiences and testimonials with your product, building authenticity for your brand. ChatGPT can provide creative ideas for engaging your audience effectively.

4. Virtual Assistant Role: Reiterating a point mentioned in previous chapters, consider incorporating ChatGPT as your virtual assistant on social media. Engage users in personalized discussions, compelling them to share meaningful conversations that contribute to your campaign objectives.

5. Data Security: As you gather customer information, prioritize ensuring its safety. Implement robust privacy and data security measures to prevent unauthorized access and safeguard customer trust.

ChatGPT has undergone significant improvements, emerging as a valuable ally in running effective ads and generating organic leads for your business. It has not only alleviated the marketing stress for many new brands and business owners but has also guided them on an optimized internet journey. The next chapter will provide insights into maximizing productivity using AI systems, offering practical guidance for leveraging these tools to their full potential

CHAPTER 10: HOW TO IMPROVE YOUR PRODUCTIVITY LEVEL USING AI

For ages, productivity has been a significant factor in achieving the best results. Imagine ticking off your to-do list, especially before the targeted time you set for yourself, bringing satisfaction and happiness. This helps you have more time and capacity to focus on other aspects of your life.

Studies have shown that good management in a workspace increases and promotes a high level of productivity, enhancing an organization's market growth and sales revenue. It can also produce excellence in the workplace and achieve overall expansion and wealth for a business.

Many people want to improve their productivity, health, and wellness and try to find balance, but they need more. Even if they decide to do other stuff besides their work, they will probably focus on their work to meet deadlines and responsibilities. The same challenge occurs in businesses, especially for startups trying to keep their business rolling, especially in their first to third year of initiating their companies.

Since the emergence of AI (Artificial Intelligence), individuals, companies, and organizations have tapped into the power of this language model to enhance productivity statuses. This has helped several businesses to get optimum results within a short period.

In this chapter, I will explain how you can also use Artificial Intelligence to boost your productivity level in your personal and business activities.

One transformative method for enhancing productivity is Automation. Through technological improvement, automation has become a powerful tool to simplify tasks and eliminate repetitive duties and functions. This has increased efficiency in work.

With the advancement of digital personal assistants, Google Assistant, and other technological tools, you can automate tedious and mundane tasks. From scheduling appointments to automating emails and programs and also controlling tasks, this has increased work efficiency. You now have more time for your family, other careers, and other activities you have been willing to do. You can also automate your budget, keep track of your finances, and help you concentrate on different aspects of life.

The same applies to organizations when they automate their workflow. It will help boost the productivity level across different branches working in the organization. Using Camunda, a platform that allows human workflows, ensures that operations concerning people operate smoothly. Camunda provides lightweight, easy-to-use models to rectify slow, inadequate, or broken human procedures. There are several others that businesses can also make use of, such as RPA, and Robotics Process Automation, which makes use of software to automate definite tasks that are repetitive. The Robotics Process Automation task is taught to imitate every repetitive human process, such as copying and pasting data into a field.

Kissflow is a business process and workflow management software that automates repetitious tasks with comfort, precision, and flexibility. This ends complex jobs, increasing business visibility and tracking the process. You can also process your data with Kissflow as well, transferring your data, and also receiving notifications.

These tools are more comprehensive than the ones stated here. You can check for other unique tools on the internet that work for your brand and start using them.

Another transformative method for enhancing productivity is Communication and Collaboration. Communication is a significant factor in building a successful business. It is an essential factor in planning and making decisions in the organization. The power of communication enables the smooth running of an enterprise. It is said that a decision or transaction can only take place in management once there is a sense of communication. That is why the major work of a manager lies in his communication skills. The manager can only convey his goals, objectives, and passions, give orders, allocate responsibility, and assess his team's performance. These boil down to the fact that nothing can be done without communication.

Collaboration, on the other hand, in a business setting, is a situation whereby people come together to achieve a common goal in the organization. Collaboration improves the way people work together and solves a specific problem. Deloitte said, "To solve the problem in a business, companies need to leverage proficiency across several industries with online and integrated collaboration tools to help employees work together as a team."

That is where the usefulness of AI (Artificial Intelligence) comes in. Artificial Intelligence tools help similar sectors in the organization, such as Data Science, Machine learning, and domain experts, to collaborate closely to design communication models. This model helps solve challenges, share knowledge, and decide how the organization can improve. The collaborative platform helps in the editing of code that was used, testing the model, and, most importantly, ensuring that the model created is working perfectly.

Artificial intelligence enables virtual workspaces where people in different units can work together on a project, share documents, and communicate effectively to ensure the team's advancement. Several artificial Video conferencing tools like facial recognition, computerized translation, and transcription will improve the communication experience. Several technologies have been put in place to enhance communication and collaboration irrespective of the location, improving the company's status.

This has allowed people to work from home, giving seamless interaction between them and their prospects, clients, or bosses. This has reduced the physical working hours of some organizations that have tapped into using these tools, generating more revenue.

Through virtual assistance and chatbots, communicating effectively is no longer a barrier. This lets you get information from other subordinates, enabling them to achieve more tasks conveniently and boost their productivity.

Artificial Intelligence also helps in Knowledge management: AI can help organize and retrieve information. This helps enable the sector to eradicate the need to direct customers to other sector towers to their challenge. However, this has allowed employees to respond to people's questions quickly.

Knowledge Management systems create vital knowledge programs for new intakes, enabling them to work in a fine-tuned environment with meager costs and learn faster and more effectively.

The knowledge base, supported by a strong knowledge management program, offers continuous learning opportunities. Onboarding and fresh agents can learn faster, resulting in a better working environment and meagerer costs. The knowledge management system also helps different teams access the same set of information, and this helps in lessen chaos among them; however, it enables them to work effectively.

Through the knowledge management system, you can fetch data from different sources. Using AI, you can incorporate data across numerous ways yet get your desired data. One of the tools organizations use is CRM (Customer Relationship Management).

Through the use of Knowledge Management, you can retain satisfied, suitable, and up-to-date content. Before Artificial Intelligence was created, information was primarily stored in a storage room, making some of it old and less valuable because people need to dispose of it or update it. AI support management maintains this information and updates it when necessary. The knowledge management system also helps collect data from different teams in a database, making it easier to retrieve when necessary, improving productivity in several sectors.

Artificial intelligence has helped several businesses initiate and enhance productivity using tools that can help them get optimal results for their companies and reduce stress, giving them access to time for other activities rather than paying all attention to their job.

CHAPTER 11: HOW TO MAKE MONEY WITH CHATGPT AND ARTIFICIAL INTELLIGENCE

Artificial Intelligence can be incorporated into several sectors across the globe. In previous chapters, I have written about how ChatGPT and AI can be used to make money in some industries worldwide. In this chapter, my focus is to talk about other sectors that I have yet to discuss and how AI revenue can be generated from them.

Agriculture:

The agricultural sector has seen a remarkable transformation by incorporating the Artificial Intelligence model. From crop monitoring to pest control, building robust economics through trade, to yield improvement and resource management. A significant Artificial Intelligence application that can transform the agriculture sector is ChatGPT. Through AI and ChatGPT, farmers, traders, and individuals involved in agricultural businesses can open new possibilities and opportunities, making essential waves in improving sales.

One benefit of using ChatGPT and Artificial Intelligence is monitoring livestock and crops. This helps farmers have a better understanding of their crops and the habitat in which they are planted. Additionally, it provides insight into the health of their crops, offering accurate and perfect information about the state of their crops, such as humidity, temperature, soil fertility, and several other factors. This helps farmers reduce operational costs and enhance productivity for maximum results.

Artificial Intelligence can also help farmers prevent crop diseases and predict the condition of the crop. Through AI algorithms and ChatGPT, farmers can expect early signs of crop disease and receive information on how to prevent the infections from spreading. This will surely help farmers avoid expensive losses owing to crop diseases.

Weather forecasting plays a vital role in specifying farming techniques and minimizing risks. By incorporating artificial intelligence tools, you can predict and receive real-time weather updates, allowing adjustments to irrigation schedules during drought conditions and putting in place protective standards before erosion, storms, and other tragic experiences that can affect the crop. This has enhanced the agricultural sector to generate more sales while minimizing risks.

Energy Industry:

The energy industry is becoming more sustainable all over the world. With the aid of Artificial Intelligence and ChatGPT, there is much improvement in the energy sector. The language model can improve energy efficiency by identifying trends and patterns through which energy usage is optimized. This helps the industry lessen wastage, reducing expenses.

Investing in energy schemes is irresistible as the world moves towards a more sustainable future. You can use ChatGPT to plan and develop your project if you are in the energy industry. It can also help you assess several factors affecting energy, such as wind habits, geographical information, and other considerations, to get more ideas about locations for renewable energy installation. With all these resources, you can determine profitable investment opportunities in the energy sector and monitor real-time data from the energy system using ChatGPT.

By implementing proactive maintenance strategies based on ChatGPT's insights, companies can optimize asset performance, reduce costly breakdowns, and maximize revenue generation. Artificial Intelligence could predict the lifespan of clean energy systems and improve the recycling of materials used in the energy system, such as solar panels. The language model lets you know the best materials to recycle the substances, organizing efficient ways to store and dump. AI also helps maintain and repair renewable energy, minimizing risks and improving the safety of individuals. AI also helps in predicting the probability of natural disasters like hurricanes, floods, and volcanic eruptions to minimize harm to the clean energy system, indicating other things needed to maintain the energy system to keep it proactive.

One significant way to make money through energy systems is by taking advantage of market fluctuations. The algorithm can help automate trading findings and research so you don't have to monitor the market constantly. This will help you buy energy when prices are low, and you can sell it back when they fluctuate.

Food Industry:

The food industry is one of the fastest-growing businesses globally. It is well said that AI technology is used more often in the industry, from producing food to processing the food, packaging the food to food waste, safety, and even the delivery process; Artificial Intelligence is used. If you run a local restaurant, you can invest in AI tools for upgrading and building new perceptions of your brand.

One of the ways you can make AI is to collect information from your customers or even a new set of people so that you can know how they want their food. Some love their food spicy and salty, while some don't. Artificial Intelligence will help you know precisely what they want and serve them the best. Customers give the best reviews when they are satisfied with what they eat.

ChatGPT can generate new recipes your customers would love to try. ChatGPT doesn't require writers to research essential and exciting dishes you can make. This also saves you money while you make more money. Using ChatGPT, you can make food based on dietary constraints to meet the specific needs of your customers. This will help people with food allergies strategize their food and give you more information about what they would love and wouldn't like.

Another way you can make money through ChatGPT is by starting your blog as a chef. You can explain procedures, processes, and results to people, asking them for feedback to improve your culinary skills. You can make more money monetizing your blog; use ChatGPT to get content ideas.

Consulting Business:

Another way to make money is by offering consulting services to people. In simple terms, consultation provides specific solutions to different individuals in your specialization while they pay you for it. Consultants charge an average of $45 to $150 per hour, depending on your level of expertise. It is said that Consultants who use Artificial Intelligence are most likely to be replaced by those who don't. However, you must be careful when using these technological tools for your business.

ChatGPT and other AI models have been abused; many people think they can be used for anything because these language models can't replace your level of expertise but can only refine it. The results from these models are different from your own experience. In consulting, experience goes a long way. It would be best to know about leveraging these tools. It is of utmost importance. The essence of ChatGPT is to generate content for your brand, optimize your brand, and make your work faster and less stressful.

ChatGPT and other AI models have been abused; many people think they can be used for anything because these language models can't replace your level of expertise but can only refine it. The results from these models are different from your own experience. In consulting, experience goes a long way. It would be best to know about leveraging these tools. It is of utmost importance. The essence of ChatGPT is to generate content for your brand, optimize your brand, and make your work faster and less stressful.

Artificial Intelligence can be a valuable asset in consultancy, aiding in data analysis, trend prediction, and providing insights that enhance decision-making processes. However, it's crucial to remember that AI is a tool to complement human expertise rather than replace it entirely.

This chapter emphasizes the diverse applications of AI across different industries, showcasing how businesses can leverage this technology to enhance efficiency, minimize risks, and tap into new revenue streams. Whether it's in agriculture, the energy sector, the food industry, or consultancy, the integration of AI, including ChatGPT, opens up innovative possibilities for growth and success.

The continuous advancement of AI technology provides a dynamic landscape for businesses, encouraging them to adapt and explore new avenues for development. As we delve deeper into the potential of AI in various sectors, the opportunities for revenue generation and operational improvement become increasingly evident.

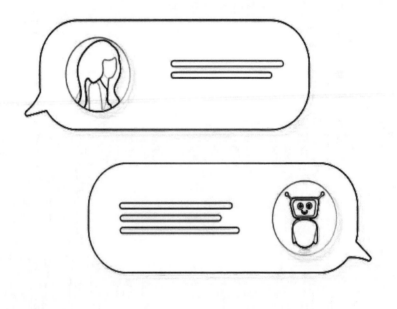

CHAPTER 12: INNOVATIVE CHATBOT APPLICATION FOR REVENUE APPLICATION

Chatbots stand out as sophisticated tools used for both personal and business purposes, transforming how we engage with companies and organizations since their inception in the mid-1960s.

Revenue applications, designed to simplify revenue processes and enhance legal decision-making, play a pivotal role in streamlining business operations. Widely employed in banks and larger companies, these applications facilitate sales processes.

The integration of Chatbots into Revenue applications serves to enhance customer accessibility, strengthen relationships, and manage complex tasks efficiently. In essence, Chatbots contribute significantly to business expansion.

Through this integration, organizations can adeptly handle large volumes of customer queries simultaneously, ensuring swift responses. Chatbots enable delightful and pleasant conversations with multiple individuals while maintaining the tone and voice of the brand. Leveraging chatbots in branding and revenue activities has a positive impact on customer engagement.

As known, Chatbots are adept at collecting data, encompassing preferences, purchasing behaviors, and various other factors. This information becomes instrumental for revenue applications to target the right audience with compelling offers, thereby updating sales techniques and potentially leading to increased sales.

An intriguing application of Chatbots in revenue applications involves utilizing Artificial Intelligence algorithms to offer diverse pricing choices and discounts. Dynamic pricing chatbots, for instance, analyze inventory levels and adjust prices accordingly, mitigating demand and supply instabilities. This results in a more efficient industry operation by reducing overstocking and stockouts challenges.

Furthermore, Chatbots play a crucial role in purchase restoration, contributing to sales and income generation. They ensure every user experiences excellent customer service, aiding in securing sales. Innovatively, Chatbots solicit customer feedback and reviews, providing valuable insights for businesses to address concerns, upgrade services, and meet customer expectations, thereby contributing to revenue generation.

Implementing Chatbots in revenue applications also ensures real-time information delivery to customers, promoting transparency that encourages repeat business and drives revenue growth. Additionally, Chatbots act as strategic problem solvers, allowing organizations to respond promptly to challenges, thus preventing potential setbacks.

For those reliant on organizations offering financial planning services, incorporating chatbots into apps proves beneficial. This enables the creation of personalized financial planning services encompassing budgeting, debt management, and retirement preparations.

In the realm of financial institutions, Chatbots serve various roles, from monitoring transactions to detecting compliance violations, thus preventing fines and preserving the institution's reputation. They aid in rendering wealth management services by analyzing customer data and providing recommendations based on financial objectives and risk tolerance.

Furthermore, Chatbots streamline the loan application process by automating lengthy cycles, providing guidance and support to customers. Financial institutions benefit from the efficient gathering of customer information, enabling accurate predictions and strategic decision-making in loan approvals.

Intelligent Chatbot and Generative AI

The synergy between Chatbots and Artificial Intelligence (AI) heralds a new era of innovation, particularly with the integration of generative AI. In this dynamic landscape, these technological advancements continue to redefine how businesses engage with customers, streamline operations, and foster growth.

AI-Enhanced Chatbots:

The marriage of Chatbots with AI elevates their functionality to new heights. AI empowers Chatbots with the ability to interpret user queries more intelligently. This not only enhances the accuracy of responses but also enables Chatbots to learn from each interaction, continuously improving their conversational capabilities.

In revenue applications, this advanced AI integration equips Chatbots with the capability to analyze customer behavior at a profound level. By deciphering patterns in preferences, purchase history, and interactions, AI-driven Chatbots assist in crafting highly targeted and personalized experiences. This, in turn, contributes to more effective sales strategies and heightened customer satisfaction.

Moreover, AI enables Chatbots to navigate complex decision-making processes. Whether it's recommending products, adjusting pricing dynamically, or assisting in intricate financial transactions, AI-driven Chatbots act as intelligent assistants, enhancing efficiency and precision.

Generative AI Integration:

The integration of generative AI, with Chatbots at the forefront, brings an element of creativity and natural language understanding to the conversation. Generative AI models, like ChatGPT, developed by OpenAI, add a layer of sophistication to Chatbots' language capabilities. This allows them to generate human-like responses, making interactions more natural and engaging.

In revenue applications, the inclusion of generative AI enables Chatbots to craft nuanced and contextually relevant responses. They can engage users in dynamic conversations, providing not only solutions to queries but also generating creative content that aligns with the brand's voice. This personalized and human-like interaction contributes significantly to building stronger customer relationships.

Generative AI also plays a pivotal role in content creation for marketing and branding within revenue applications. By leveraging ChatGPT and similar models, businesses can automate the generation of compelling copy, promotional material, and even creative product descriptions. This not only saves time but ensures a consistent and appealing brand presence across various communication channels.

The Power of Integration:

When both AI and generative AI are seamlessly integrated into Chatbots, the result is a versatile tool that goes beyond conventional customer interactions. In revenue applications, this advanced Chatbot becomes a multifaceted asset, capable of not only addressing queries and facilitating transactions but also crafting persuasive narratives and engaging content.

This integrated approach extends into analytics and insights. AI-driven Chatbots, armed with generative capabilities, can analyze vast datasets to extract meaningful patterns and trends. This empowers businesses to make informed decisions, refine their strategies, and stay ahead in the competitive landscape.

Looking Ahead:

As technology continues to evolve, the integration of AI and generative AI into Chatbots will play an increasingly pivotal role in shaping the future of customer engagement and revenue generation. The ability to provide intelligent, creative, and personalized interactions positions businesses at the forefront of innovation, fostering customer loyalty and driving sustainable growth.

CHAPTER 13: IDENTIFYING PROFITABLE OPPORTUNITIES: THE PASSIVE INCOME WITH CHATGPT

Persuasive income is sweet! Imagine earning money from activities you're not actively involved in daily, all thanks to the system you've already put in place. Sweet, right? This means you can have multiple sources of income without hiring a SINGLE PERSON. And yes, ChatGPT has made the process easier and faster. In this chapter, I will show you how to use the Machine Learning model ChatGPT to generate passive income without stressing yourself. Let's dive into it.

One of the best ways you can use ChatGPT to generate a profitable income is by creating digital products such as ebooks and online courses. The beautiful thing is that you can use a chatbot to get multiple ideas on how to create the course and, most importantly, several strategies for selling the book. For example: If you want to write a book in a particular niche, log into your ChatGPT and input the correct prompt. ChatGPT can help you with the best headlines for your book; all you have to do is edit them to avoid plagiarism. Let's give it a try.

My prompt: Write several compelling headlines for my book on the importance of investing. "ChatGPT:"

- "Unlocking Wealth: The Ultimate Guide to Harnessing the Power of Investing."

- "Investing for the Future: The Key to Financial Freedom and Prosperity"

- "From Rags to Riches: How Investing Transforms Lives and Fortunes."

- "The Millionaire Mindset: Embrace Investing and Supercharge Your Wealth"

- "Investing 101: Master the Art of Building and Growing Your Financial Empire."

- "Unleashing the Power of Compound Interest: The Investment Secret to a Lifetime of Wealth."

- "Investing Unveiled: Your Path to Financial Independence Starts Here."

- "The Wealth Builder's Blueprint: Strategies and Insights for Successful Investing."

- "Investing: Your Passport to a Secure and Abundant Future."

- "The Investment Revolution: Empowering Individuals to Take Control of Their Financial Destiny."

Remember, these are just headlines. You can customize and expand upon them to create engaging chapter titles or subheadings that further explore the importance of investing in your book. Look at all these. With these beautiful headlines, you can pick one that resonates better with your audience. Then, ChatGPT can also help you develop different chapters that you can modify to your taste. Let's check that out, also.

Let's pick a topic from one of those responses. I prefer Number 3, "From Rags to Riches: How Investing Transforms Lives and Fortunes." Here is my prompt: Write several captivating chapters I can come up with for my book: From Rags to Riches: How Investing Transforms Lives and Fortunes." "ChatGPT:

Chapter 1: The Spark of Ambition

In this opening chapter, we delve into the life of a humble protagonist whose dreams are ignited by a chance encounter. From a modest upbringing in a small town, they witness the power of investing firsthand through a captivating story or a successful entrepreneur. Inspired by this tale of economic transformation, our protagonist becomes determined to explore the world of investing and discover how it can change their life.

Chapter 2: The Quest for Knowledge

With newfound determination, our protagonist embarks on a quest for knowledge. They immerse themselves in books, attend seminars, and connect with experienced investors. From learning the fundamentals of the stock market to understanding the intricacies of real estate, our protagonist's thirst for knowledge knows no bounds. Along the way, they encounter mentors who share invaluable insights, shaping their understanding of the investment landscape.

Chapter 3: The First Leap

Armed with knowledge, our protagonist takes their first leap into investing. Whether investing in stocks, starting a small business, or purchasing their first property, this chapter showcases the excitement and trepidation of the first investment. We witness the risks, the sleepless nights, and the leap of faith that propels them forward, all while highlighting the potential rewards that await those willing to take calculated risks.

Chapter 4: Triumph and Setbacks

In this chapter, our protagonist experiences both triumphs and setbacks. They encounter a significant win in the stock market but face unexpected challenges, such as a market downturn or a failed business venture. This chapter showcases the resilience required to navigate the ups and downs of the investment world. Through these experiences, our protagonist hones their investment skills, learning valuable lessons that will shape their future decisions.

Chapter 5: The Power of Patience

As our protagonist continues their investment journey, they discover the power of patience. This chapter explores the importance of long-term investment strategies, whether in stocks, real estate, or other assets. We witness our protagonist's growing ability to weather market fluctuations and resist the allure of short-term gains. This chapter also introduces the concept of compounding, illustrating how patient investing can lead to exponential growth over time.

Chapter 6: A Fortuitous Encounter

In this captivating chapter, our protagonist crosses paths with a mysterious and successful investor. This encounter leads to an unexpected mentorship and opens doors to exclusive investment opportunities. Our protagonist gains insights into unconventional investment strategies and discovers the potential for extraordinary returns. This chapter highlights the transformative power of networking and the influence of critical relationships on one's investment journey.

Chapter 7: Making a Difference

As our protagonist's wealth grows, they begin to explore the impact they can make beyond their gain. This chapter delves into their philanthropic endeavors and pursuing investments that align with their values. Whether supporting social causes, investing in sustainable technologies, or funding educational initiatives, our protagonist discovers the profound satisfaction of using their wealth to make a positive difference in the world.

Chapter 8: Legacy and Generational Wealth

In the final chapter of this captivating journey, our protagonist reflects on their transformation from rags to riches and contemplates their legacy. They explore the notion of generational wealth and the responsibility that comes with it. This chapter delves into the importance of financial education for future generations and the role of investing in securing a prosperous future. Our protagonist realizes that their journey is about personal wealth and leaving a lasting impact on future generations.

By crafting each chapter with engaging storytelling, practical insights, and emotional resonance, your book "From Rags to Riches: How Investing Transforms Lives and Fortunes" will captivate readers and inspire them to embark on their investment journey." This is stunning. ChatGPT didn't just help me with the lists of chapters I could develop and a summary of what each chapter should contain.

However, you can use ChatGPT to write each chapter of the book while you edit to your audience's tone and voice. With ChatGPT, you can write a good book in less than 24 hours. CharGPT can also help you with different marketing schemes and platforms. You can sell your book, automate the process, and sell while focusing on other things. Let's try it out on ChatGPT to see the result. My prompt: Write me several strategies on how I can sell my ebook online and also automate the sale process "ChatGPT:

Selling an ebook online can be an effective way to generate income and reach a broad audience. To automate the sale process and maximize your sales, consider implementing the following strategies:

- Choose the right platform: Select a platform specializing in ebook sales, such as Amazon Kindle Direct Publishing (KDP), Smashwords, or Gumroad. These platforms provide built-in tools and distribution channels to help you reach your target audience.

- Create an engaging landing page: Build a dedicated landing page for your ebook where you can provide a compelling description, cover image, testimonials, and any other relevant information. Include a clear call-to-action to encourage visitors to make a purchase.

- Optimize your website for conversions: Optimize your website by placing prominent and visually appealing buttons or banners that lead visitors to the ebook's sales page. Use persuasive copywriting techniques and offer limited-time discounts or bonuses to increase conversions.

- Utilize email marketing: Set up an automated email marketing campaign to capture the email addresses of potential buyers. Offer a free chapter or bonus content in exchange for their email, and then send them a series of emails that promote your ebook, share testimonials, and highlight its benefits. Consider automating the process with an email marketing platform like Mailchimp or ConvertKit.

- Leverage social media: Utilize social media platforms like Facebook, Twitter, Instagram, or LinkedIn to promote your ebook. Create engaging posts, share valuable content related to your book's topic, and include links to your sales or landing pages. Consider running targeted ads to reach a larger audience.

- Collaborate with influencers: Identify influencers, bloggers, or experts in your ebook's niche and reach out to them for potential collaborations. Offer them a free copy of your ebook and ask if they would be willing to write a review, feature your ebook in a blog post, or share it with their audience. Their endorsement can significantly boost your sales.

- Offer affiliate partnerships: Set up an affiliate program where other individuals or businesses can promote your ebook in exchange for a commission on each sale they generate. Use affiliate marketing platforms like ClickBank, ShareASale, or Amazon Associates to automate the affiliate tracking and payment process.

- Provide bonuses or extras: To incentivize potential buyers, offer additional bonuses or extras along with your ebook. These could include exclusive access to a private Facebook group, a companion workbook, video tutorials, or templates. Automate the delivery of these bonuses upon purchase to enhance the customer experience.

- Implement a secure and automated payment system: Choose a reliable payment gateway, such as PayPal, Stripe, or Gumroad, to handle the payment process securely and automatically. These platforms often provide customizable checkout options and integrate easily with ebook-selling platforms.

- Optimize for search engines: Conduct keyword research and optimize your sales page or landing page for search engines. By targeting relevant keywords in your content, meta tags, and headings, you can improve your ebook's visibility in search engine results and attract organic traffic.

Remember to monitor and analyze your sales and marketing efforts regularly. This will help you identify the most effective strategies and refine your approach to maximize sales and further automate the process." ChatGPT just helped in writing and rendering help on how I can sell my ebook without hiring anybody. Digital products are what ChatGPT can help you with in any sector. I deliberately make use of digital products so that you can understand better. As long as you enter the appropriate prompts, ChatGPT is ready to help you with all your problems and troubles and excitedly scale your business. It would be best if you tried it out today. Remember, the result is in the implementation. Go Win!

CHAPTER 14:   The 10 Types of Generative AI & How They Work

Persuasive potential is truly fascinating! Picture effortlessly unraveling the intricacies of Generative AI, unlocking a realm where innovation converges with intellect. Exciting, isn't it?

This means you can explore various facets of Generative AI without delving into intricate technicalities. And yes, ChatGPT is here to simplify this process for you. In this chapter, I'll guide you through the diverse landscape of Generative AI, breaking down its types and unveiling the wizardry behind each. Let's delve into it.

One of the finest approaches to comprehend Generative AI is by understanding its diverse types and functionalities. Just like crafting compelling headlines for your book, you can utilize ChatGPT to unravel the nuances of each type. For instance, if you wish to demystify the world of Generative AI, prompt ChatGPT to elucidate the various types and their operations. Let's give it a try.

- **Text Generation Wizards**

"Crafting Prose: The Magical Wordsmiths of Generative AI."

"Literary Alchemy: How Text Generation Wizards Transform Ideas into Language."

"Beyond Words: The Artistry of Text Generation and Creative Expression."

- **Image Artisans**

"Pixel Perfection: Understanding the Canvas of Image-Generating AI."

"From Code to Canvas: How Image Artisans Bring Imagination to Life."

"Visual Symphony: The Harmonious Blend of Algorithms and Aesthetics."

- **Music Maestros**

"Melody in Mathematics: Exploring the World of AI-Generated Music."

"Harmony of Algorithms: Unraveling the Composition Skills of Music Maestros."

"AI Symphony: Composing Notes in the Digital Age."

- **Coding Conjurers**

"CodeCraft: The Enchanting Powers of AI in Writing Code."

"Syntax Sorcery: Decoding the Magic of Coding Conjurers."

"Binary Alchemy: How AI Transforms Ideas into Executable Spells."

- **Poetry Pioneers**

"Verses in Voltage: Illuminating the Poetry of Generative AI."

"Rhyme and Reason: Navigating the Art of Poetry Pioneers."

"Poetic Algorithms: The Rhythmic Dance of Words in Generative Poetry."

- **Design Dreamweavers**

"Pixels in Progress: Designing Realities with AI Dreamweavers."

"Graphic Symphony: The Visual Poetry of Design Generated by AI."

"Visualizing Code: How Design Dreamweavers Translate Algorithms into Art."

- **Conversation Choreographers**

"Dialogues in Data: The Conversational Craft of AI Choreographers."

"Speechcraft: Unraveling the Magic Behind Conversation Choreography."

"Virtual Discourse: Navigating the Terrain of AI-Generated Conversations."

- **Game World Architects**

"Pixel Realms: Building Worlds with Generative AI in Gaming."

"Virtual Vistas: The Architectural Prowess of Game World Generators."

"Gaming Alchemy: How AI Shapes Interactive Universes."

- **Scientific Scribes**

"Data Dialogues: The Scientific Language of AI-Generated Research."

"Algorithmic Papers: Deciphering the Scripts of Scientific Scribes."

"From Data to Dissertation: How AI Narrates Scientific Discoveries."

- **Recipe Renderers**

"Culinary Code: The Recipe for AI-Generated Gastronomic Delights."

"Taste Bytes: The Art of Culinary Creations by AI Recipe Renderers."

"Edible Algorithms: Exploring the Palate of AI-Generated Recipes."

Remember, these are just glimpses into the vast spectrum of Generative AI types. You can tailor and expand upon them to create engaging chapters or subheadings that delve into the enchanting world of Generative AI. Analyze these, select the types that resonate with your curiosity, and let's explore how ChatGPT can unravel the mechanics behind each type.

Stay tuned as we embark on a journey to demystify the realm of Generative AI, one algorithmic masterpiece at a time."

This enthralling exploration of Generative AI is just the beginning, much like the captivating journey we've undertaken with investing. Let's continue the narrative and uncover the magic that unfolds when algorithms and creativity converge.

Unraveling the mystique of Generative AI tools is akin to discovering a treasure trove of digital artisans, each weaving a unique tapestry of creativity. Just like selecting captivating chapters for your book, choosing the right Generative AI tools is crucial for unleashing the full potential of this transformative technology. In this exploration, I'll guide you through the enchanting realm of the ten best Generative AI tools, shedding light on their prowess and the wonders they can craft:

- **Text Blaze: The Word Weaver**

Crafting Prose with Precision

Text Blaze stands as a maestro in generating captivating narratives, transforming ideas into eloquent expressions. Its ability to understand context and weave intricate sentences makes it an invaluable tool for content creators and wordsmiths.

- **Deep Dream Generator: The Visionary Illustrator**

Dreamlike Visualizations Unleashed

Much like an artist's dream, Deep Dream Generator transforms images into surreal, almost fantastical creations. Its deep neural networks reimagine visuals, creating a harmonious blend of reality and imagination.

- **AIVA: The Melodic Muse**

Symphonies Composed by Algorithms

AIVA is the virtuoso of AI-generated music, composing melodies that resonate with emotion. Its adaptive learning capabilities enable it to craft musical pieces across genres, elevating the realm of AI-generated music.

- **OpenAI Codex: The Code Conjurer**

Deciphering the Syntax Sorcery

OpenAI Codex is a coding conjurer, translating ideas into executable spells. Its prowess in understanding and generating code makes it a powerful ally for developers, streamlining the coding process with an infusion of AI magic.

- **Poem Generator: The Rhyme Reveler**

Verses Crafted in Voltage

Much like a poet's muse, the Poem Generator dances with words, creating verses that evoke emotion. Its rhythmic prowess in generating poetry showcases the poetic side of Generative AI, captivating audiences with its literary charm.

- **Artbreeder: The Visual Alchemist**

Design Realities with Pixel Magic

Artbreeder emerges as a design dreamweaver, allowing users to blend and create visuals that transcend the ordinary. Its intuitive interface empowers users to explore the vast landscape of AI-generated art.

- **ChatGPT: The Conversation Choreographer**

Dialogues Orchestrated in Data

ChatGPT, the conversation choreographer, navigates the nuances of virtual discourse. Its ability to generate contextually relevant and coherent conversations makes it an invaluable tool for chatbot development and interactive AI interfaces.

- **GANPaint Studio: The Game World Architect's Canvas**

Pixel Realms Painted with Precision

GANPaint Studio redefines the canvas for game world architects, allowing them to paint intricate details and landscapes. Its generative abilities contribute to the creation of immersive gaming universes.

- **SciGen: The Scientific Scribe**

Algorithmic Papers Deciphered

SciGen emerges as a scientific scribe, transforming data into comprehensible research scripts. Its contribution to automating the generation of scientific papers showcases the evolving landscape of AI in research.

- **RecipeVA: The Culinary Code Culminator**

Edible Algorithms and Gastronomic Delights

RecipeVA stands as the culinary code, crafting recipes that tantalize the taste buds. Its ability to generate innovative and delectable recipes showcases the fusion of technology and gastronomy.

Remember, these tools are just a glimpse into the expansive world of Generative AI, each contributing uniquely to the creative spectrum. Dive into the magic of these tools, explore their capabilities, and witness firsthand the transformative potential they hold.

As we embark on this exploration of the finest Generative AI tools, envision the possibilities they unfold – a digital symphony orchestrated by algorithms, a canvas painted with pixelated dreams, and a world where creativity knows no bounds. Stay tuned as we unravel more chapters in the fascinating narrative of Generative AI, continuing our journey through the realms of innovation and imagination.

Essential Tools for Developing Your Own Generative AI Model:

Embarking on the enchanting journey of crafting your own Generative AI model requires the guidance of essential tools, much like a wizard relying on their trusted wand and spellbook. In this chapter, I'll illuminate the path for aspiring AI creators, unveiling the must-have tools that will empower you to shape your own magical realm of Generative AI.

- **TensorFlow: The Magic Core**

Weaving Neural Networks with Precision

TensorFlow stands as the foundational magic core for many AI creators. Its open-source nature and extensive documentation make it an ideal choice for constructing neural networks, the very essence of Generative AI.

- **PyTorch: The Luminary's Flame**

Illuminating the Path of Neural Alchemy

PyTorch, with its dynamic computational graph, serves as a luminary's flame guiding creators through the intricate process of neural alchemy. Its intuitive interface and vast community support make it a powerful ally in crafting Generative AI models.

- **Keras: The Enchanting Interface**

Simplifying Sorcery for Novice Alchemists

Keras acts as the enchanting interface, simplifying the intricacies of model creation. Its user-friendly design and seamless integration with TensorFlow empower even novice alchemists to wield the powers of Generative AI.

- **Jupyter Notebooks: The Alchemist's Diary**

Recording Spells and Observations

Jupyter Notebooks serve as the alchemist's diary, documenting every spell and observation in a comprehensible manner. Their interactive nature allows creators to experiment, iterate, and refine their models with ease.

- **GANs (Generative Adversarial Networks): The Dynamic Dual**

Conjuring Realism through Adversarial Harmony

GANs, the dynamic dual of Generative AI, pit generator against discriminator, creating a dance of adversarial harmony. Understanding and implementing GANs is essential for crafting models that generate realistic and high-quality outputs.

- **CUDA: The Acceleration Elixir**

Speeding Spells with GPU Acceleration

CUDA acts as the acceleration elixir, leveraging GPU power to expedite the spellcasting process. Its integration with frameworks like TensorFlow and PyTorch enhances the speed and efficiency of training Generative AI models.

- **Scikit-Learn: The Alchemy Assistant**

Simplifying the Elixir of Data Transformation

Scikit-Learn serves as the alchemy assistant, simplifying the elixir of data transformation. Its comprehensive set of tools for data preprocessing and manipulation eases the path for creators in preparing their datasets.

- **Matplotlib and Seaborn: The Visualization Spells**

Conjuring Visuals for Insightful Enchantments

Matplotlib and Seaborn act as the visualization spells, allowing creators to conjure insightful visuals. Understanding the art of visual representation is crucial for interpreting and refining Generative AI models.

- **GitHub: The Codex Repository**

Archiving Spells and Collaborative Magic

GitHub serves as the codex repository, archiving spells and enabling collaborative magic. Version control and collaboration are vital aspects of Generative AI development, and GitHub provides the perfect platform for such endeavors.

- **Colab: The Cloud Conduit**

Unleashing Spells in the Cloud

Colab, powered by Google, serves as the cloud conduit, allowing creators to unleash their spells in a cloud-based environment. Its seamless integration with Jupyter Notebooks provides a collaborative and resourceful space for Generative AI experimentation.

As you delve into the creation of your own Generative AI model, consider these tools as your trusted companions. Much like a seasoned alchemist with a well-worn spellbook, these tools will guide you through the magical process of shaping and refining your AI creations. With the right spells and tools at your disposal, the journey of crafting your own Generative AI model becomes an exhilarating adventure in the realms of innovation and discovery. So, ready your wand, open your spellbook, and let the magic unfold.

BONUS

<u>Unlock the power of ChatGPT prompts!</u>

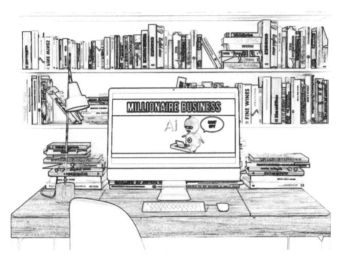

Scan the QR code now

and ignite your work with tailored solutions for every situation.
Embrace the opportunity to elevate your performance and conquer
new heights in your career. Don't wait, seize the moment and
unleash your full potential with ChatGPT!

It's a FREE BONUS ONLY FOR YOU

Made in United States
Troutdale, OR
01/06/2024

16745171R00076